T0346066

BIG ENGLISH

BIG tv

4

2ND EDITION

BIG TV WORKBOOK

Pearson Education Limited
KAO Two
KAO Park
Harlow
Essex CM17 9NA
England
and Associated Companies throughout the world.

www.English.com/BigEnglish2

First published 2017

ISBN: 978-1-292-20361-4

Set in Heinemann Roman

Printed in Italy by L.E.G.O. S.p.A.

Acknowledgements
The publisher would like to thank the following for their kind permission to reproduce their photographs:

(Key: b-bottom; c-centre; l-left; r-right; t-top)

123RF.com: ABImages 12 (carrots), Nickolay Adamiuk 28 (colored powder), 30cl, Natalya Aksenova 24 (oil lamp), Alexmillos 8 (TV commercial), Ian Allenden 37tl, Andrey Alyukhin 28br, Apinan 8 (brand), 10l, Arogant 24 (loom), Aticl2 17tc, Pavlo Baishev 23tl (claw), Blueringmedia 13 (snacks), Nadezhda Bolotina 21b (primates), Phonlawat Chaicheevinlikit 8 (billboard), Suphakit Chansaeng 13 (healthy meal), 14 (healthy meal), Chelovek 20bl (bear), Ionut David 32cl, Jose Manuel Gelpi Diaz 4 (quadruplets), 6cr, Djoronimo 17tr, Dolgachov 36 (learn a subject), Alejandro Duran 29b, Konstantin Egudin 31l, Oleg Elagin 20 (claws), 21/1, Don Faulkner 27cr, Fiphoto 8 (window display), Volodymyr Goinyk 28 (balloon ride), 30cr, Goodluz 9b, Steven Heap 32cr, Adrian Hillman 4 (quintuplets), Ruslan Huzau 36 (play snooker), Images 39c, Infinitegraphic 31cl, Eric Isselee 23tl (ears), 23tr (bat), 23tr (snake), Pavel Isupov 24/1 (gadgets), Eleonora Ivanova 19r (tomatoes), Konstantin Kalishko 23br, Igor Kardasov 33tr, Brian Kinney 12 (meats), Ljupco 8 (promotion), luislouro 15cr, 27br, 39br, Magone 12 (chicken), 15t (chicken), Vadym Malyshevskyi 28bc, Steve Mann 32bl, W.Scott McGill 27r, Nik Merkulov 33tc, Fernando Gregory Milan 8 (movie release), 10cr, Auttapon Moonsawad 32l, Teguh Mujiono 39r, Dmytro Nikitin 17r (nuts), Baiba Opule 12 (snacks), Perseomedusa 32r, Pictur123 21b (birds), Sirichai Raksue 22br, 23tr (lizard), Alexander Raths 21b (fish), Red33 39l, Sahua 13 (breakfast), Scanrail 12 (soda), 15t (soda), 25 (the internet), Antonio Balaguer Soler 36 (sing), Subbotina 12 (pasta), 15t (pasta), Sudowoodo 39cr, Tashka2000 12 (drinks), Sirikorn Thamniyom 7r, 19cl, 31br, Dinis Tolipov 29tc, 30b, Oleg Tovkach 4 (triplets), 6cl, Jiri Vaclavek 20 (skin), 21/2, 22tr, Ximagination 36 (speak a new language), PAN XUNBIN 23tl (skin), Anastasy Yarmolovich 26, Feng Yu 32bc; **Pearson Education Ltd:** Studio 8 7l, 19cr, 31bl, 39bl, Amit John 13 (lunch), Arvind Singh Negi / Red Reef Design Studio. Pearson India Education Services Pvt. Ltd 13 (dinner), Pradip Kumar Bhowal. Pearson India Education Services Pvt. Ltd 31r, Ratan Mani Banerjee. Pearson India Education Services Pvt. Ltd 31cr, Roddy Paine 4/1 (sextuplets), 4/2 (sextuplets), 4/3 (sextuplets), 4/4 (sextuplets), 4/5 (sextuplets), 4/6 (sextuplets), 6r/1, 6r/2, 6r/3, 6r/4, 6r/5, 6r/6, Tudor Photography 6b, 36 (bake a cake), Jules Selmes 9cl, 29tl; **Shutterstock.com:** 1stGallery 20 (teeth), 21/7, 22cl, 9l, 10cl, Africa Studio 17r (milk), Vlad Ageshin 32br, Matusciac Alexandru 24 (electric lights), Anetta 4 (sister), Subbotina Anna 12 (salad), 15t (salad), Artos 25 (cell phone), Nachiketa Bajaj 21cr, Bergamont 16 (peanuts), 19r (peanuts), Victor Brave 31c (boy), 31c (girl), 39cl, Steve Byland 23tr (hummingbird), Pablo Calvog 16 (headache), Sam Chadwick 24 (horse and buggy), Cobalt88 16 (pollen), 19r (pollen), Donna Ellen Colema 4 (twins), Morphart Creation 27l, CREATISTA 36 (ballet dance), Decathlon 16 (cough), Deklofenak 9r, Tiplyashina Evgeniya 16 (allergy), Iakov Filimonov 28 (tomato fight), 30l, Goodluz 37tc, Haveseen 20 (fingers), 21/3, 21c, 22tl, Images by Dr. Alan Lipkin 23bc, Eric Isselee 20br (monkey), Matej Kastelic 18b, Natalia Klenova 13t (packed lunch), 14 (packed lunches), KMW Photography 4 (identical twins), 6l, Patryk Kosmider 20 (ears), 21/4, 22cr, Ksander 24/2 (gadgets), 25 (laptop), James Laurie 16 (runny nose), Lightspring 13 (junk food), 14 (junk food), Lucky Business 5t, 28 (couple), Milos Luzanin 24 (phone), Alexey Malashkevich 8 (advertising), 10b, Mattia Menestrina 5bl, Mettus 12 (crisps), Michaeljung 4 (parents), 37tr, Holly Miller-Pollack 20 (throat), 21/5, 23tl (throat), Monkey Business Images 13t (warm dish), 14 (warm dish), 14b, 33b, Nadino 5br, Nattanan726 21b (reptiles), 23bl, Nattika 17r (eggs), 18tl, Sergey Novikov 11l, 23cr, 35l, Oksana2010 18tr, M. Unal Ozmen 12 (chocolate), Pakhnyushcha 24/3 (gadgets), Pavel L Photo and Video 37b, Phase4Studios 4 (brother), Popartic 17r (tomatoes), 18cl, Andrey Popov 9cr, 10r, Ppart 24 (oven), Pressmaster 21cl, Racobovt 17r (fish), RimDream 36 (play chess), Elena Schweitzer 12 (candy), Selins 33tl (pottery), Umberto Shtanzman 25 (apps), Earth planet globe map. The Earth texture of this image furnished by NASA. (http://visibleearth.nasa.gov/view_rec.php?id=2430) 28 (planet Earth), Earth planet globe map. The Earth texture of this image furnished by NASA. (http://visibleearth.nasa.gov/view_rec.php?id=2430) 28bl, Natalia Siverina 34, Lloyd Smith 25b, Stefanolunardi 28 (environment), Sukharevskyy Dmytro (nevodka) 8 (product), Marina Sun 38, T.Karanitsch 20 (neck), 21/8, Tobik 12 (rice), Evlakhov Valeriy 20bl (fish), Repina Valeriya 12 (grains), Vangert 23tr (goldfish), Stephen VanHorn 24 (tracking device), visivastudio 20 (fin), 21/6, 23tl (fin), Valentyn Volkov 12 (vegetables), Tom Wang 11r, 23cl, 35r, Wavebreakmedia 28 (dance to music), 30r, 33tl (guitar lesson), Tracy Whiteside 15cl, 27bl, Darren Whittingham 16 (fur), 18cr, 19r (fur), Lisa F. Young 17tl, Yuris 29tr

All other images © Pearson Education

Contents

1 Twins

I will learn about families with many siblings.

1 Listen, number, and say.

 twins

 identical twins

 triplets

 quadruplets

 quintuplets

 sextuplets

 parents

 brother

 sister

2 Choose a word from 1. Write.

a A boy who has the same parents as you. _____

b Two people who look exactly the same. _____

c Your mother and father. _____

d Six people born at the same time. _____

e A girl who has the same parents as you. _____

f Two people born at the same time. _____

g Three people born at the same time. _____

h Five people born at the same time. _____

3 **Listen, look, and say.**

personality

jolly

serious

4 **Think of a brother, a sister, or another family member. Are you similar or different? Tell a partner. Complete.**

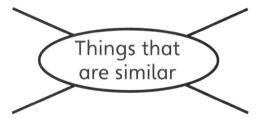
Things that are similar

Things that are different

5 **Now think of a friend. How are you similar? How are you different? Tell a partner.**

6 ▶ⓥ **Watch. Check (✓) what you hear or see.**

☐ identical twins ☐ triplets ☐ quadruplets ☐ sextuplets

7 ▶ⓥ **Watch again. Write True or False.**

a 24 twins attend a school in Honduras. _____

b Sometimes twins swap and sit exams for each other. _____

c Twin Month is celebrated in Beijing. _____

d All of the sextuplets are from one multiple birth. _____

🎧8 **Read and circle. Then listen and check.**

Everyone in your class is different. Everyone has different **schools / families**, physical features, and personalities. But sometimes, there are exceptions. If you have a pair of **twins / teachers** in your class, they will share the same home, **parents / cats**, and birthday … and if there are identical twins, they will look **the same / different**, too!

9 **Follow the lines. Ask and answer with a partner.**

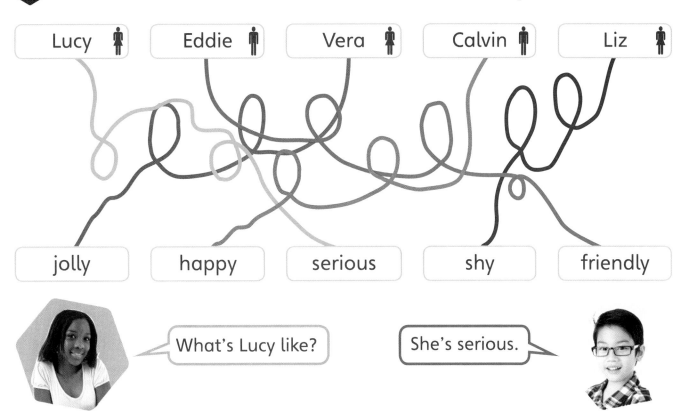

| Lucy | Eddie | Vera | Calvin | Liz |

| jolly | happy | serious | shy | friendly |

What's Lucy like?

She's serious.

10 **Write and match. Then listen and check.**

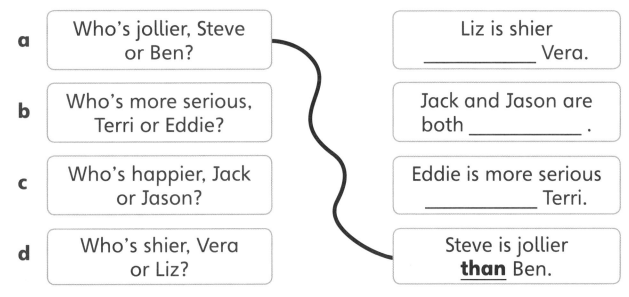

a Who's jollier, Steve or Ben?

b Who's more serious, Terri or Eddie?

c Who's happier, Jack or Jason?

d Who's shier, Vera or Liz?

Liz is shier _____ Vera.

Jack and Jason are both _____ .

Eddie is more serious _____ Terri.

Steve is jollier **than** Ben.

THINK BIG What are you like? What are your classmates like?

Buy! Buy! Buy!

I will learn about advertising.

 1 **Listen, number, and say.**

☐ advertising

☐ billboard

☐ window display

☐ brand

☐ promotion

☐ movie release

☐ product

☐ TV commercial

2 **Choose a word from 1. Write.**

a A window in a store showing products for sale. _____

b The name of a product. _____

c Something that is made to be sold. _____

d A new movie to watch at the movie theater. _____

e An advertisement shown on television. _____

f A large sign used for advertising. _____

g Advertising to tell people about a product. _____

③ 🎧 **Listen, look, and say.**

company

department
store

customer

movie fans

④ **How often do you do these things? Can you remember any advertisements in these places? Complete with a partner.**

How often do you ...	Names of advertisements
take the bus? _____	_____
watch TV? _____	_____
read a magazine? _____	_____
go online? _____	_____
visit a store? _____	_____

⑤ **What TV commercials do you like? Why? Tell a partner.**

6 ▶_{v2} **Watch. Check (✓) what you hear or see.**

☐ brand   ☐ companies   ☐ movie release   ☐ customers

7 ▶_{v2} **Watch again. Answer the questions.**

a Is it expensive to advertise on the LED billboards? _____

b In New York, how do they attract customers in the winter?

_____

c Which movie did the film company want to promote?

_____

d Do the fans like *The Simpsons* store? _____

e Why does the London store play music to its customers?

_____

8 🎧 **Read and circle. Then listen and check.**

Companies pay a lot of **time / money** to have their **advertisements / movie releases** lit up around big cities. The **windows / billboards** are often iconic. It's **easy / expensive** for companies to advertise here. In New York, they use window displays to attract customers in the winter. There's an actress in this **shop window / TV commercial**. And this window has an interactive **display / mirror** for people to take selfies.

9 **Follow the lines. Ask and answer with a partner.**

Eva — watch a TV commercial — three times a week

Sam — shop for food — every day

Ina — go shopping for clothes — once a month

Zac — go to a movie release — twice a year

How often does Eva go to a movie release?

She goes to a movie release once a month.

10 **Where can you see these advertisements? Circle.**

1 Girls' sandals, half price today!

 a bookstore
 b toy store
 c shoe store

2 Buy your tickets to see *Ice Age* here!

 a movie theater
 b clothes store
 c the dentist

3 Visit our amazing new art exhibition!

 a swimming pool
 b museum
 c clothes store

4 All jump ropes, only $2!

 a movie theater
 b toy store
 c shoe store

THINK BIG Think of a TV commercial or an advertisement you dislike. Why don't you like it? Tell your classmates.

3 School Food

Before You Watch

I will learn about different foods at school.

9

1 Listen, number, and say.

☐ candy

☐ potato chips

☐ soda

☐ pasta

☐ chocolate

☐ carrots

☐ chicken

☐ rice

☐ salad

2 Complete the table. Categorize the foods from 1.

meats	vegetables	drinks	grains	snacks

(3) Listen, look, and say.

packed lunch

warm dish

healthy meal

junk food

4 What food do you have in your country? Talk to a partner. Write.

breakfast

_____

_____

lunch

_____

_____

dinner

_____

_____

snacks

_____

_____

5 What food can you eat in your school? Do you like it? Tell a partner.

6 ▶(v3) **Watch. What do you hear or see? Number the pictures in order, 1 to 4.**

☐ healthy meal

☐ junk food

☐ packed lunches

☐ warm dish

7 ▶(v3) **Watch again. Write True or False.**

a Some schools serve breakfast and lunch. _____

b Chinese students get pasta with their warm dish. _____

c Jamie Oliver is a famous soccer player. _____

d Healthy food helps performance in class. _____

8 **Read and circle. Then listen and check.**

Some children bring **cooked / packed** lunches from home. But they have to remember not to pack any junk food. They can't bring **salad / candy**, **carrots / potato chips**, sodas, or chocolate. Of course, we like our food to be **horrible / tasty** as well as healthy.

9 Follow the lines. Ask and answer with a partner.

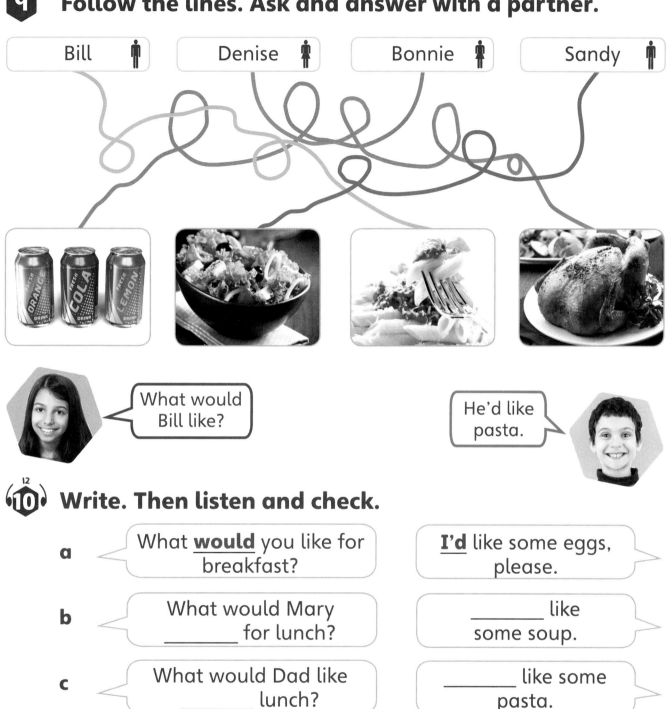

Bill 👤   Denise 👤   Bonnie 👤   Sandy 👤

What would
Bill like?

He'd like
pasta.

10 Write. Then listen and check.

a   What **would** you like for breakfast?   **I'd** like some eggs, please.

b   What would Mary _____ for lunch?   _____ like some soup.

c   What would Dad like _____ lunch?   _____ like some pasta.

d   _____ would the children like for dinner?   _____ like some rice.

THINK BIG What foods would your classmates like for dinner? Make a chart.

How Do You Feel?

I will learn about allergies and their remedies.

 1 Listen, number, and say.

☐ headache

☐ runny nose

☐ cough

☐ allergy

☐ peanuts

☐ pollen

☐ fur

2 **Read and complete.**

> fur   pollen   headache   cough   allergy

a Judy has a terrible pain in her head. She has a _____.

b Max has an _____ to tomatoes. He can't eat pizza or tomato salad.

c Jane has a cold and an awful _____.

d The _____ from these flowers is making me sneeze!

e I'm allergic to some animals' _____, particularly cats.

3 Listen, look, and say.

search for a treatment

develop a cure

suffer from hay fever

4 What food allergies do you know? Order the letters and write. Then match.

a m k l i _____

b t n u s _____

c g s e g _____

d a t o m o t s e _____

e i h f s _____

5 Do you have any allergies? Tell a partner.

I suffer from Hay fever. It gives me a runny nose.

6 ▶v4 **Watch. What do you hear or see? Number the pictures, 1 to 4.**

7 ▶v4 **Watch again. Write True or False.**

a Bhavna is allergic to milk. _____

b Lena suffers from pollen allergy. _____

c Garret is allergic to peanuts. _____

d Many children are allergic to peanuts. _____

e Doctors can't find a cure for some allergies. _____

f Lena now eats a few peanuts every day. _____

8 🎧15 **Read and choose. Then listen and check.**

Scientists are always looking for **allergies / treatments**. In the 1980s, a **British / headache** inventor thought of bubbles to protect hay fever sufferers from **pollen / fur**. However,

the bubbles were very uncomfortable, so the remedy **was / wasn't** very successful. Today, scientists are developing real solutions and even a **symptom / cure** for some allergies.

9 Follow the lines. Ask and answer with a partner.

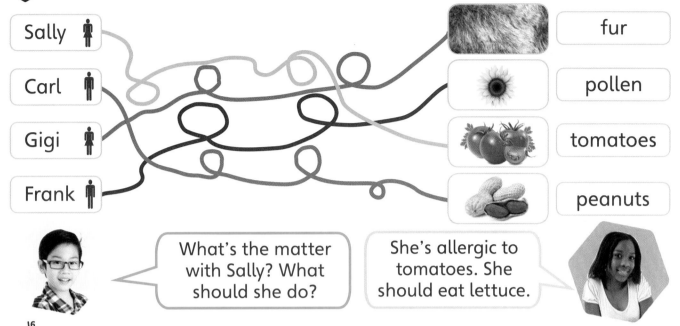

Sally	fur
Carl	pollen
Gigi	tomatoes
Frank	peanuts

What's the matter with Sally? What should she do?

She's allergic to tomatoes. She should eat lettuce.

16 🎧 10 Read, choose, and write. Then listen and check.

Hay Fever: The Facts

Hay fever is [1] **an** allergic reaction with symptoms similar [2] _____ a cold. It makes you feel horrible because you have a [3] _____ nose and itchy eyes. The main cause of hay fever is pollen, [4] _____ other causes can be cigarette smoke or strong perfume. What can you do about hay fever? Firstly, you [5] _____ speak to your doctor to find the best remedy for you. You may need to take [6] _____ medicine or even have an allergy test.

1	a / (an) / any	**4** but / well / never
2	from / with / to	**5** shouldn't / should / can't
3	sneeze / runny / cold	**6** any / some / an

THINK BIG

What should people do who have allergies? What should other people do to help? Tell your classmates.

Weird and Wonderful Animals

Before You Watch

I will learn about unusual animals.

1 🎧 17 **Listen, number, and say.**

☐ claws	☐ skin	☐ fingers	☐ ears
☐ neck	☐ fin	☐ teeth	☐ throat

2 **Label the pictures. Use the words from the box.**

fingers   teeth   claws   fin   skin   neck   ears

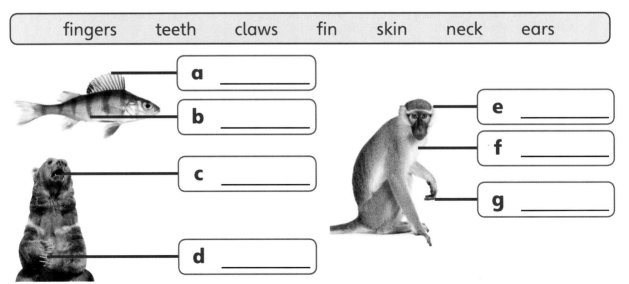

a _____

b _____

c _____

d _____

e _____

f _____

g _____

3 Look, read, and choose. Then listen and check.

1 sharp / thin
claws

2 long / scaly
skin

3 sharp / thin
fingers

4 big / red
ears

5 red / long
throat

6 scaly / tiny
fins

7 sharp / tiny
teeth

8 scaly / long
neck

 4 Listen, look, and say.

cute

strange

fierce

5 What strange animals do you know? Complete.

primates	fish	reptiles	birds
_____	_____	_____	_____
_____	_____	_____	_____
_____	_____	_____	_____

6 What famous animals are there in your country? Tell a partner.

7 ▶(V5) **Watch. What do you hear or see? Number the pictures in order 1 to 4.**

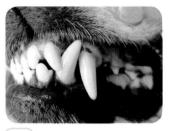

☐ thin fingers   ☐ sharp teeth   ☐ big ears   ☐ scaly skin

8 ▶(V5) **Watch again. Write True or False.**

a The aye-aye is a primate with long fingers. _____

b Frigate birds have sharp claws. _____

c Archer fish live in the Amazon. _____

d The gliding lizard has sharp teeth. _____

e The gliding lizard is a type of dragon. _____

 9 **Read and write. Then listen and check.**

| sharp | teeth | lizard | fly | Indonesia | strange | wings |

There's a reptile that is very _____.
It has _____ claws and scaly skin. Its
skin stretches to form _____ and it
has sharp _____. But it isn't a dragon,
and it doesn't breathe fire! It's a gliding
lizard, and it lives in _____. It can't
_____ but it can glide from tree to
tree. And it only eats insects. Perhaps it was this little _____
that inspired ancient legends of fierce dragons!

10 **Follow the lines. Ask and answer with a partner.**

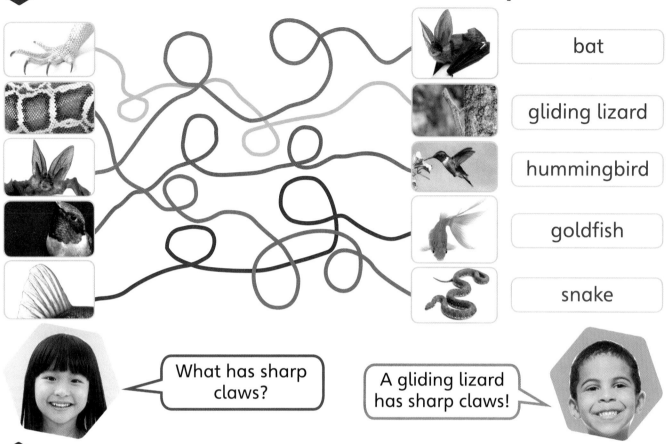

bat

gliding lizard

hummingbird

goldfish

snake

What has sharp claws?

A gliding lizard has sharp claws!

11 **Write a description of two of these animals. Use the words in the box to help you.**

sharp claws   scaly skin
thin fingers   big ears
a red neck   sharp teeth
a long throat

a The _____ has _____ and _____.

It _____.

b The _____ has _____ and _____.

It _____.

 **What's your favorite unusual wild animal? Can you describe it?**

Low-tech Life

I will learn about old technologies.

 1 Listen, number, and say.

☐ oil lamp

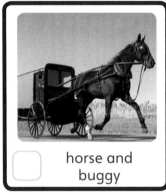

☐ horse and buggy

☐ gadgets

☐ oven

☐ loom

☐ electric lights

☐ phone

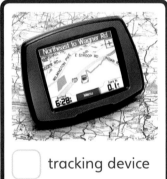

☐ tracking device

2 Choose a word from 1. Write.

a   A gadget which helps you to find something. _____

b   A light made from burning fuel. _____

c   A type of transport. _____

d   A machine used for cooking. _____

e   A machine used for making cloth. _____

f   A device for talking to other people. _____

22
3 Listen, look, and say.

the Internet

apps

laptop

cell phone

4 How did people use to live? Talk with a partner.
Complete.

There were no washing machines, so people used to
_____.

There was no TV, so people used to
_____.

There were no cars, so people used to
_____.

There were no cell phones, so people used to
_____.

There were no electric lights, so people used to
_____.

5 What old technology do your grandparents still have?
Ask and answer with a partner.

6 ▶ⱽ⁶ **Watch. What do you hear or see? Number the items in order 1 to 6.**

☐ the Internet   ☐ apps   ☐ cell phone

☐ oil lamps   ☐ a horse and a buggy   ☐ looms

7 ▶ⱽ⁶ **Watch again. Complete.**

old technology	new technology
_____	cell phone
_____	electric light
_____	modern car
_____	modern oven
_____	machines in factories

8 🎧²³ **Read and complete. Then listen and check.**

oven	car	machines	oil	technologies

The _____ began as a horse and a buggy. The first motor cars needed a little help to get started. They had _____ lamps for headlights, and their wheels were made out of the metal, iron, rather than rubber. But some _____ have stayed the same over hundreds, and even thousands, of years. The Maasai people have continued to cook with pots on a fire, rather than an _____. They also make very good-quality blankets without high-tech _____.

9 **Look at objects people used at different times in the past. Ask and answer with a partner.**

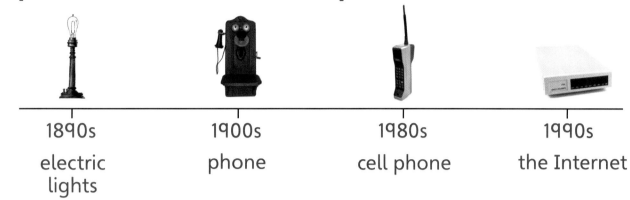

1890s	1900s	1980s	1990s
electric lights	phone	cell phone	the Internet

Did people have the Internet in the 1900s?

No, they didn't. But they did have phones.

24
10 **Write a verb from the box in the correct form. Then listen and check.**

> listen   use   use   listen   ~~have~~   do   use   travel

a Did people **have** tracking devices 30 years ago?

No, they _____. But they did have maps.

b Did your grandmother _____ to music on an MP3 player as a child?

No, she didn't. No one had that gadget then! They _____ to the radio.

c Did office workers _____ computers 50 years ago?

No, they didn't. They _____ typewriters.

d Before cars, how did people use to _____ to work?

They _____ to travel by horse and buggy.

THINK BIG

What technology could you not live without? Why? What new technology can you imagine in the future?

7 Global Festivals

I will learn about different festivals and special days.

1 Listen, number, and say.
25

☐ dance to music

☐ colored powder

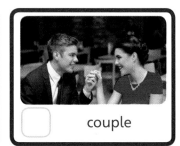
☐ couple

☐ planet Earth

☐ tomato fight

☐ balloon ride

☐ environment

2 What could you do on these special days? Write expressions using verbs from the box and words from 1.

> protect   throw
> dance   take   look after

Earth Day

a _____   b _____

Festivals

c _____   d _____

Valentine's Day

e _____

3 Look and write. Then listen, check, and say.

celebrate	participants

_____   _____

4 What festivals do you know? Talk with a partner. Complete.

local festivals
_____
_____
_____

global festivals
_____
_____
_____

5 How can you celebrate Earth Day? Tell a partner.

6 ▶v7 **Watch. What do you hear or see? Number the pictures in order 1 to 4.**

☐ tomato fight

☐ colored powder

☐ balloon ride

☐ dance to music

7 ▶v7 **Watch again. Write True or False.**

a La Tomatina is a festival from Spain. _____

b During La Tomatina, people throw colored powder. _____

c Holi festival is celebrated in summer. _____

d In India, the festival participants dance to music. _____

e Valentine's Day is celebrated all over the world. _____

8 🎧27 **Read and complete. Then listen and check.**

| planet   family   environment   April |

A special day that is celebrated around the _____ is Earth Day. It is celebrated on _____ 22nd. It reminds us to appreciate our planet Earth and to look after the _____. In the Philippines, people come every year to clear waste plastic from beaches. As well as the environment, special days remind us to also appreciate friends, _____, and our world.

9 **Follow the lines. Ask and answer with a partner.**

| in April | next month | in February | in spring | this summer |

When are you going to give a card?

I'm going to give a card in February!

28

10 **Read and complete with going to. Then listen and check.**

| have | go | go | meet |

a When are you going to have your birthday party?

I'm **going to have** it on Saturday, the sixth.

b When are they going to the music festival?

They're _____ next week, on the first.

c When are you going to meet your friends?

We're _____ them tomorrow.

d When is Bill going to Colombia?

He's _____ there on June 11th.

THINK BIG

What festival are you going to celebrate soon?

8 What's Your Hobby?

I will learn about different hobbies.

 1 Listen, number, and say. *29*

☐ matchsticks

☐ dolls

☐ royal objects

☐ sculptures

☐ models

☐ locket

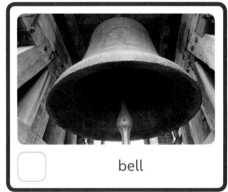
☐ bell

2 Choose a word from 1. Write.

a Things used for making fire. _____

b Something which makes a loud ringing noise. _____

c Things made for celebrating a king or queen. _____

d A necklace with a small picture inside. _____

e Small toys which look like real objects and places. _____

f Art objects made from stone, wood, or clay. _____

3 Listen, look, and say.

hobbies

collecting things /
a collection

metal detecting

4 What hobbies do you know? Talk with a partner. Complete.

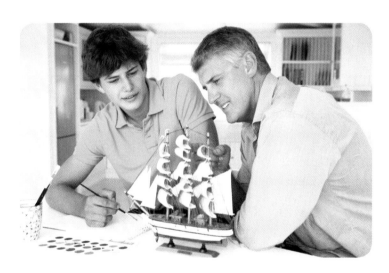

Which hobbies can you do inside?	Which hobbies can you do outside?
_____	_____
_____	_____
_____	_____

5 What do you or a family member collect? Ask and answer with a partner.

6 ▶ⓥ⑧ **Watch. Check (✓) what you hear or see.**

☐ hobbies   ☐ collecting things   ☐ royal objects

☐ dolls   ☐ sculptures   ☐ model

☐ matchsticks   ☐ metal detecting   ☐ locket

7 ▶ⓥ⑧ **Watch again. Answer and write.**

| 6,000 | 500 | 3 million | 3,600 | 10,000 |

a How many royal objects does the lady have? _____

b How many dolls has the man collected? _____

c How much did the most expensive doll cost?
_____ Singapore Dollars.

d How old is the golden locket? _____ years old.

e What is the value of the locket? _____ US Dollars.

8 🎧³¹ **Read and circle. Then listen and check.**

In England, a little boy called James started metal **detective / detecting**. When he was only **thirteen / three**, he found something very special. James found a golden locket in his **house / garden**. It's 500 years old! James doesn't quite understand, but the golden **shell / locket** could be worth three **million / thousand** US dollars!

9 **Follow the lines. Ask and answer with a partner.**

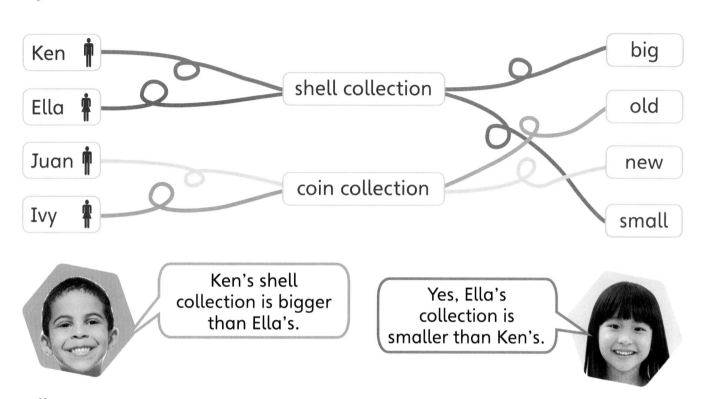

Ken — shell collection — big
Ella — shell collection
Juan — coin collection — old
Ivy — coin collection — new / small

> Ken's shell collection is bigger than Ella's.

> Yes, Ella's collection is smaller than Ken's.

10 **Match. Then listen and check.**

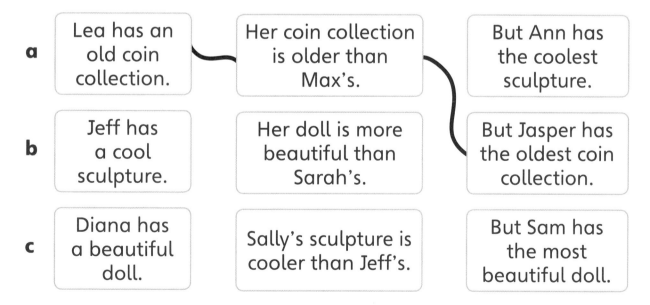

a Lea has an old coin collection. — Her coin collection is older than Max's. — But Ann has the coolest sculpture.

b Jeff has a cool sculpture. — Her doll is more beautiful than Sarah's. — But Jasper has the oldest coin collection.

c Diana has a beautiful doll. — Sally's sculpture is cooler than Jeff's. — But Sam has the most beautiful doll.

THINK BIG

Museums have big collections of things. What interesting collections can you see at a museum near you?

q Skills and Talents

I will learn about trying new things.

 1 **Listen, number, and say.**

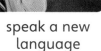

speak a new language

play snooker

ballet dance

learn a subject

play chess

sing

bake a cake

2 **Choose a word or phrase from 1. Write.**

a I passed my Spanish exam! I can _____.

b She dances on her toes. She can _____.

c His cooking skills are great. He can _____.

d She's good at board games. She can _____.

e Give her the microphone – she can _____.

3 Look and write. Then listen, check, and say.

| graduate from college | win a scholarship | have an online video call |

_____   _____   _____

4 How can you learn new skills? Talk with a partner. Complete.

What skills can you learn ...		
from a teacher?	by yourself?	from a book?
_____	_____	_____
_____	_____	_____
_____	_____	_____

5 What skills and talents do you have? Ask and answer with a partner.

6 ▶vq **Watch. Check (✓) what you hear or see.**

☐ bake a cake ☐ have an online video call ☐ listen to music ☐ read books

☐ play chess ☐ graduate from college ☐ ballet dance ☐ play snooker

7 ▶vq **Watch again. Complete.**

name	personal information	skill
Timothy	_____	_____
Phiona	_____	_____
Greg	_____	_____
Faakhir	_____	_____
Wang Wuka	_____	_____

8 35 **Read and complete. Then listen and check.**

| smartest | video | mathematics | 14 | college |

Greg Smith is _____ and is sometimes called the _____ kid in the world. He has already graduated from _____ and is now doing advanced studies in _____. He was also nominated for the Nobel Peace Prize when he was 12, for advocating children's rights. In his free time, he likes to play _____ games and basketball.

9 **Follow the lines. Ask and answer with a partner.**

Mia · Alfredo · Selina · Franklin · Connie

> What would Mia like to learn?

> She'd like to learn how to ballet dance.

36
10 **Write and match. Then listen and check.**

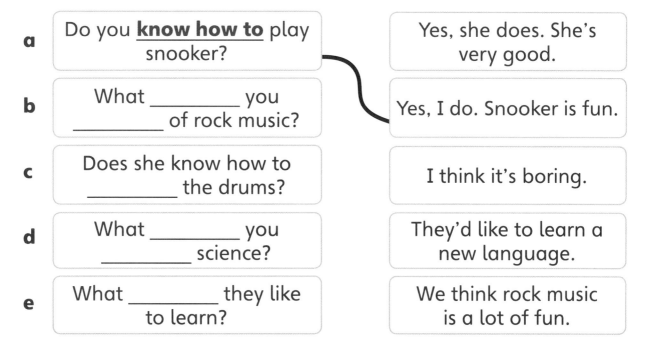

a Do you **know how to** play snooker?

Yes, she does. She's very good.

b What _____ you _____ of rock music?

Yes, I do. Snooker is fun.

c Does she know how to _____ the drums?

I think it's boring.

d What _____ you _____ science?

They'd like to learn a new language.

e What _____ they like to learn?

We think rock music is a lot of fun.

What skills do you think are important for winning a scholarship? Which are important for graduating from college?

Word List

❶ Twins

brother
identical twins
parents
quadruplets
quintuplets
sextuplets
sister
triplets
twins
friendly
happy
jolly
personality
serious
different
similar

❷ Buy! Buy! Buy!

advertising
brand
billboard
company
customer
department stores
movie fans
movie release
product
promotion
TV commercial
window display
every day
once a month
three times a week
twice a year
go shopping for clothes
go to a movie release
shop for food
watch a TV commercial
bookstore
movie theater
museum
shoe store
swimming pool
toy store

❸ School Food

candy
carrots
chicken
chocolate
pasta
potato chips
rice
salad
soda
healthy meal
junk food
packed lunch
warm dish
breakfast
dinner

lunch
drinks
grains
meats
snacks
vegetables

❹ How Do You Feel?

allergy
cough
fur
headache
peanuts
pollen
runny nose
develop a cure
search for a treatment
suffer from hay fever
eggs
fish
milk
tomatoes
hay fever

❺ Weird and Wonderful Animals

claws
ears
fin
fingers
neck
skin
teeth
throat
big
cute
fierce
long
red
scaly
sharp
strange
thin
tiny
birds
fish
primates
reptiles
bat
gliding lizard
goldfish
hummingbird
snake

❻ Low-tech Life

electric lights
gadgets
horse and buggy
loom
oil lamp
oven
phone
tracking device
apps
cell phone
laptop
the Internet
factories
machines
modern car
modern oven
washing machine

❼ Global Festivals

balloon ride
colored powder
couple
environment
music
planet Earth
tomato fight
celebrate
participants
global festivals
local festivals

❽ What's Your Hobby?

bell
dolls
locket
matchsticks
models
royal objects
sculptures
collecting things / a collection
hobbies
metal detecting
coin
shell

❾ Skills and Talents

bake a cake
ballet dance
learn a subject
play chess
play snooker
sing
speak a new language
listen to music
play video games
read a book
graduate from college
have an online video call
win a scholarship